Colourless Green Ideas Sleep Furiously

Colourless Green Ideas Sleep Furiously

Short Essays and Alternative Versions

Mark Frutkin

QUATTRO BOOKS

The publication of *Colourless Green Ideas Sleep Furiously* has been generously supported by the Canada Council for the Arts and the Ontario Arts Council.

Cover design: Diane Mascherin
Cover image: Holly Briesmaster
Author's photo: Sandra Russell
Typography: Grey Wolf Typography
Editor: Allan Breismaster

Library and Archives Canada Cataloguing in Publication

Frutkin, Mark
      Colourless green ideas sleep
furiously / Mark Frutkin. -- 1st ed.

Issued also in electronic format.
ISBN 978-1-926802-96-1

      I. Title.

PS8561.R84C65 2012   C814'.54   C2012-900339-5

Published by Quattro Books Inc.
89 Pinewood Avenue
Toronto, Ontario, M6C 2V2
www.quattrobooks.ca

Printed in Canada

Dedicated to my mother,
Anabel Elizabeth Frutkin
9 October 1919 – 31 December 2011

"All the decisive blows are struck left-handed."
– Walter Benjamin, *One-Way Street*

"Roaring dreams take place in a perfectly silent mind."
– Jack Kerouac, *The Scripture of the Golden Eternity*

Fragments of a story

Story is what we use to conjure order out of chaos.

We charm chaos into narratives that replicate and reflect established perceptions of reality.

Though it appears to be nothing but fragments, the world is in fact a unified field: of cities, thoughts, food, language, dreams, bodies, hopes, fears and passions. The unifying factor is story, the ongoing whisper we hear in our heads, the tale we tell ourselves, no more real than any other story, a play we imagine, a dream we dream.

Left-handed blows and roaring dreams

Left-handed blows are ideas that tear vents in the facade of accepted reality. They blow convention to smithereens. They knock the entire universe exactly one foot to the left – or the right. Left-handed blows have nothing to do with politics, and yet politics is controlled ultimately and entirely by left-handed blows.

Left-handed blows come from Rimbaud, Basho, Benjamin, Apollinaire, Joyce, Kerouac, Lao Tzu, Beckett, Trungpa, Eliade, Whitman, Gautama, Molly Bloom, Li Po, Emma Bovary and many others known and unknown. They come from crazy people, enemies, allies, lovers. From the sun and moon, from the planets and stars, up from under the earth.

Left-handed blows come like lightning, like water, like dreams. Left-handed blows sometimes curve all the way around and appear to come from the right. In any case, left-handed blows always come from the void, from the far reaches of the dusty nebulae, from inside the chest.

They are magnificent, astonishing, ultra-simple, silent and empty. Left-handed blows are beyond interpretation, even this interpretation.

Roaring dreams, meanwhile, are not separate from perfectly silent mind. They are the purest indication that perfectly silent mind is prowling about, a leopard in the jungles of night.

Roaring dreams are continuous like a river, like breath, like change. Roaring dreams thread in and out of time, double back, leap ahead.

When they disappear we remember them, before they come we long for them. Roaring dreams roar loudest when the silence is strong. When the silence grows weak, roaring dreams cannot be heard.

As soon as roaring dreams are noticed, they change, as if a chameleon were wired to the foreground rather than the background.

Left-handed blows only hit you when you aren't looking.

Roaring dreams only arise when mind rests in perfect silence.

Boredom

Is there anything we fear more than boredom?

Boredom, it turns out, is our only hope.

Wittgenstein said there were only the variables of reality, the details, with no unifying factor behind them. But, the groundlessness that humans glimpse when they are bored, the nothing they fear, is indeed that unifying factor.

Boredom is our only hope because it is precisely the place where new things are illuminated and born. That emptiness, that space, is the locus of the creative, it allows all possibilities. Without it, nothing is possible. Wonderfully empty and terrifying, the leap into the abyss. The source of left-handed blows and roaring dreams.

The letter A

The alphabet is a profoundly adaptable and fecund system. What tales can be told from the assembling and orchestration of twenty-six letters and a space!

The letter A was originally drawn as an ox-head (Proto-Sinaitic pictograph, 1500 B.C.). Turn the capital letter A over and one sees the prongs of the ox's horns. How it evolved (literally 'turned') from a pictograph of an ox-head to an A is a development that can be followed in the evolution of Proto-Canaanite script.

In its etymological sources, the word 'ox' suggests fertility. It derives from the Sanskrit '*uksati*', he emits semen. The Indo-European root is '*ugw*', to make wet.

Turn the ox horns upside down and one sees a rudimentary plow. At the end of nomadic cultures in the Near East, with the founding of cities and the beginnings of agriculture and written language, it is fitting that the alphabet had an ox leading the way.

(A further connection between language and bovines: the earliest Chinese writing is found on oracle bones, the shoulder blades of cattle. The bones were poked with hot branding irons and the ensuing cracks read for prophecies which were then engraved on the shoulder blades in the form of early Chinese pictographs.)

The connections between the ox and written language appear again in the form of Greek writing called boustrophedon (*bous* = ox) in which the line moves left to right and then right to left on the succeeding line, going down the page as a farmer would plough a field.

The etymological connections grow ever more intriguing when one considers that one of the sources of the word *verse* is the Middle Latin *versus*, a furrow. This conjures the image of a ploughed field that resembles a poem on the page, and vice-versa.

Evolution of the letter A: from a Proto-Sinaitic pictograph of an ox-head (1500 BC) to the modern character.

(Calligraphy by Paul Hayes.)

Letters ubiquitous

We glimpse letters everywhere: the H in the ladder and the fence, the S-bend in river and road, the alphabet on the telephone keypad, in the tangled garden, in the limbs of bodies walking the crowded street. The taps pour out letters in foaming chaos, so too do letters fly from the banner whipping in the wind. The Tibetans believe prayer flags, when fluttering in the breeze, release over and over the prayers printed on them. Cars and buses release sounds that represent alphabetic nonsense. Every mouth has a balloon attached, a bubble filled with words. Another balloon stretches and swells inside our heads. The three electric wires passing over my back yard are a lined page waiting to be filled in. The city is a kind of text, Borges' infinite library broken free of restraint and gone mad, as if the letters and words have been liberated and come pouring out of the neo-classical building like inmates released from an asylum. The letters are a kind of god: ubiquitous and omnipresent. Like a primal foundational energy, they magnetize themselves, gather, cluster, resonate, creating an ongoing story of infinite complexity.

Questions and answers

Space is an attitude, a state of mind. Space the locus of creation, a void that is charged and potent. The creative begins with space. For the visual artist, space is the empty canvas. For the musician, space is silence. For the writer, space is the blank page – terrifying, voluptuous, irresistible.

We begin with an open mind. Beginning means refining and honing the question. If you come to a final and definitive conclusion – an answer – the space fills up with that conclusion and nothing more is possible.

The question that is asked is alarming and amazing because there is both danger and possibility. If there were no danger there would be no possibility.

But let us not forget about space – left-handed space filled with roaring dreams: if you try to describe space, it fills up with your words and is gone. Turning it over, it looks the same on the bottom as on top. It is always waiting and ready, charged and candescent.

Language as social consensus

Language is determined by social consensus. We agree that the sounds "win-dow" are the apertures in the house you can see through, and "pa-per" is what you hold in your hands when reading. The sounds, in and of themselves, mean nothing. We have agreed, society has agreed, that these sounds have meaning and we are inoculated with this code from birth, by hearing our parents, our siblings and our world speak. We are both nurtured and trapped in the nexus of meaning.

Our perceptions of reality as well are controlled by social consensus, and our ultimate limitations are defined by it. In subtle and profound ways that involve complete immersion in a cultural and linguistic atmosphere, we receive and pass on the codes and definitions of so-called reality. Artists stretch those limits, tyrants and madmen break them, everyone else ignores them by living inside them.

The letter B

The pictographic source for the letter B is a house. The Indo-European root for the word 'house' means 'to cover or to hide'. Certainly, one of the functions of the house to this day in many traditional societies is to hide women and girls from the eyes of the outside world. The pictograph itself is much like a simple diagram of a walled space with a single opening, a door or a window. One can still glimpse a suggestion of this today in the letter B: turned on its flat edge, it resembles a rounded hut of two rooms.

City life, agriculture, written language – how strange that they all started roughly in the same period. As if language is written into the walls, the dwelling places, the ordered streets and squares. The city and the tilled field become, literally, a kind of text. This world speaks in a different way than it spoke to the nomad, whose ear was tuned to the cry of the jackal, the rumble of coming weather, the singsong of the headman's tales. Written language offers its user a certain kind of power and control, but something too is lost.

And yet, an echo of the oral tradition remains. These letters, these oxen and houses, have their sounds. They also speak. The letter A is a vowel – the mouth is open when the letter is voiced. The letter B is softly spat from closed lips. Open fields, closed houses.

Colourless green ideas sleep furiously

"Colourless green ideas sleep furiously." The famous linguist Noam Chomsky meant this to represent a phrase that sounded like English, had the flavour and structure of English syntax, but made no sense.

For me, however, the phrase is a concise and poetic definition for dreaming.

Charming chaos

Language ultimately is a tool – an extremely useful, even a wonderful tool, that we use to 'charm chaos'. By 'charm chaos' I mean we use language quite literally without thinking, to control the ultimate chaos behind things. Chaos, in this context, is considered as Babel, complete lack of communication, primal disorder. We charm chaos through this system of language and perception.

Language easily becomes habitual. The words slip into their neural grooves – those wrinkles in the brain – and follow their usual well-worn paths. Still, it is possible to break free from the habitual use of language, to realize and contemplate the fact that any particular language is based on an unspoken consensual agreement and is merely a tool, however extraordinary.

Our view of reality, too, is based on a cultural agreement. In other words, your view of reality may be a product of your culture. We are all acculturated to a lesser or greater degree.

To realize and experience the depth of this acculturation can result in two states of mind, similar on the surface but at opposite extremes.

On the one hand, at the confused extreme, the belief that reality is as you imagine it can be termed psychosis or delusion. The mad live in their own worlds often with their own languages. At the other extreme lies the world of the shaman or the mystic who realizes that we all create our own worlds in any case. Shamans and mystics – sometimes writers and artists can work that edge as well – create alternate worlds and yet usually remain capable of functioning in the world of accepted reality.

In this view, the distinction between fact and fiction, between myth and reality, between story and ordinary life, begins to break down.

Sacred and profane

For the so-called primitive mind, the story is real. In fact, reality *is* a story, life is the enactment of a ritualized story. And in this ritual, everyday objects are sacred – no distinction is made between the sacred and the profane. The bowl, the grain in the bowl, the song sung to the gods while grinding the grain, and the overarching sun are all sacred because they are part of the story, embodiments of myth, both transcendent and mundane.

It is intriguing to consider what happened when primitive culture pervaded Western Europe early in the twentieth century, when cultural anthropologists such as Durkheim and Malinowski returned from exotic locales in Africa and New Guinea with their eyewitness reports. They wrote not only about the mating habits of the peoples there, but discussed their 'primitive' perceptions of reality, their views of the world.

This idea brought back from aboriginal cultures – that there was no distinction between the sacred and the profane – captivated the European artists and writers of the day. Suddenly the objects of traditional, classical poetry – the tombs, angels, fountains and flowers of the Victorians of England and many other European poets who preceded them – changed into the objects of the modern mundane world: the cigarettes, gas works and automobiles of Apollinaire and the Surrealists. The result was that Picasso dared to paint *Les Demoiselles d'Avignon* using five Barcelona prostitutes as models and stuck a real piece of chair caning and a theatre ticket into a work of art.

(Of course, Caravaggio, much maligned by the Victorians, was a precursor of this approach with one crucial difference: Caravaggio used courtesans as models for religious figures whereas Picasso used prostitutes *as* prostitutes.)

Somehow, the Western world flipped the primitive view around and said, *all is profane and nothing is sacred*, rather than realizing that the sacred and profane were identical. This state of mind helped foster the breakdown of traditional institutions in the West for good and ill: monarchies were buried forever, institutional religion lost much of its power (the Jesuits were thrown out of France early in the twentieth century), and the family began a slow but profound evolution.

The West came to believe this and this alone: *Nothing is sacred.* The horrors of the past century stand as a symbol for the West's embracing of this view. Two world wars, the holocaust and the atom and hydrogen bombs are testaments to this belief. How did we make the leap from "no distinction between the sacred and the profane" to "nothing is sacred?"

Seeing how our view of reality is limited might aid us in understanding this leap and help us envision a realm where the sacred and profane come together. This is the possibility that enchanted some artists early in the twentieth century: the idea that the imagination, the power of story, could recreate the world. As in any shamanistic endeavour, there was danger. Little did they know that one imagination driven to recreate the world would be Hitler's.

Beckett's way

Samuel Beckett's way is a road of 'diminishing possibilities'. He finds fewer and fewer subjects to talk about and is finally left amazed by the fact that he is 'still alive' and can prove it only by continuing to spew forth language. His way is a spiral turning in, going ever deeper into the heart of a contradiction, into the black hole of thought and reflection and self-reference. And it is astonishing what resonance he can find there.

I prefer to 'include' everything, the entire world in its ever-increasing fertility, in its mycelium of connections. If a thing is in the world, it must connect to every other thing. I follow the way of ever-increasing, ever-multiplying possibilities. The work and the world (and all anti-worlds, as well, including Beckett's) are not separate; somehow everything points to and speaks of everything else. It is delicious chaos held together by a soft silk thread. Order shooting through the world in spasms of radiance.

The mycelium of inclusion is not Beckett's no-time no-place, nor is it Joyce's City of Dublin on a specific date – it is everywhere connected and all times at once, it is the rain forest reflected in a bassoon, it 'includes' and resonates with openness, it is so crowded with the world that it demands vast infusions of space to allow it room to dance, to tremble. It is not merely the spiral unwinding outward but a soft explosion of the always-new, the always-being-born. It disregards subtraction and lusts after nth powers. It grows and takes in the darkness and illuminates it. And ultimately it embraces irony, because all this richness, this feast of life, is empty, and includes emptiness, and feasts on emptiness even as it feasts on the world.

The story

I do not believe that literature can *make* a difference. I believe literature *is* the difference. The stories we tell not only reflect our lives but embody those lives in that they define our myths. We are living the story. The tale lends the life its definition, defines its borders, its limits, and measures its depth.

The story captures the chaos and frames it in a mirror.

Aphorisms 1

When it comes to reality, you have to believe it to see it.

Beware those who never reveal a doubt.

The common man knows just enough about modern art to have been inoculated against it.

Soul/Subconscious

What we once knew from the depths of the soul, a man or woman of our times would ascribe to the subconscious. The soul suggests a different order of reality, while the subconscious merely points to another level, slightly under the skin, a subcutaneous awareness.

Soul is a northern word, Norse, Germanic, Anglo-Saxon, the source of myth within us. *Subconscious*, on the other hand, comes from the Latin *scire*, 'to know', and is cognate with *science*.

Troy imagined

At the height of the Victorian era, the amateur German archaeologist Heinrich Schliemann found Troy VIIa, proving that the Trojan Wars were not fable but a part of history, that the shield of Odysseus rang in the brilliance of real light, and Hector's legs hugged the back of a breathing horse.

Certain scholars today question these findings. The historical veracity of the Trojan Wars is again under suspicion. I do not wish to become embroiled in this scholarly argument, but I would like to explore what this might suggest.

What we have here, in the back and forth between the fact and fiction of Troy and the Homeric epic (some of our earliest literature) is, quite literally, the profound power of the imagination, its ability to breathe life into matter. For thousands of years a city of men and women peopled human imagination. For thousands of years, listeners heard the words of Homer, assembled the stone blocks of Troy in their imaginations, limned the face of Helen, struck the shields of a thousand warriors.

The tale had power. Its roots thrust ever deeper into the human fabric, into human soil. Each listener who heard or told the tale added to its depth, its profundity. One day a chiselled piece of half-buried stone appeared on the plains of northwestern Asia Minor, not far from the waves of the Thracian Sea breaking over and over on the shore like lines of text.

A portion of wall appeared out of the earth. This happened long before Schliemann arrived. A helmet with a skull inside glinted for a moment in the sun, then was covered by dust moved by near and distant winds.

And still people listened to the tale. Fathers told sons and daughters, older brothers told younger. People heard the tale repeat itself inside their own heads, listened to their own imaginations taking life.

Meanwhile, the city of ruins was assembling itself on the plains. Tarnished shields appeared and poked out of the earth. Shards of pots, layers of paving stones, the point of a spear, all appeared and sank again under generations of soil and dust. Troy was imagined into existence and prepared for Schliemann's coming.

A trader passed nearby once and saw nothing, though he sensed a certain power in the region and fine words rose to the surface of his mind as he rode by.

We end in silence

We end in silence. There is irony in that. We who babble and shout to the ends of the earth. We end in silence. Ours is the age of irony because we choose to speak despite the knowledge that all ends in silence.

The letter D

The stylized image of a fish is the pictographic source of the letter D, a complex symbol that was later simplified into a triangle. The triangle itself (the 'delta' in Greek) later gave its name, supposedly due to its shape, to the marshy area at the mouth of the Nile River, and thus to all river mouths. A delta's fertile waters teem with aquatic life of all sorts. It seems likely that the delta was named, not after the triangle, but after the earlier fish pictograph.

Pacific

Perhaps we should entertain the notion that we really have come to the end. We stand and look out on the Pacific. Nowhere to go. Nowhere left to discover. All has been done. The snake has bitten its tail. The newborn has eaten its mother, the present has swallowed the past and forgotten everything.

Chair

A picture may be worth a thousand words, but the worth of a word is limited only by the imagination. Take the word 'chair' for instance.

When I say 'chair' you might imagine a fine cherrywood seat in an elegant dining room, the dirty white plastic chairs in the back yard, a king's throne, a slab of stone. The possibilities are legion. You might think of the chair you found your aunt slumped in the night she died, patterned with faded roses. You might think of a chair on the *Titanic*, a chair at the United Nations, an electric chair, your child's first wooden seat. When you hear the word 'chair', you might think of the same word in Italian, French, Serbian, Urdu, Mandarin. You might think of the history of chairs, the construction of chairs, chairs as art, as objects to throw, to prop against a door, to stand on when changing a light bulb or reaching into a high cupboard for dusty muffin tins. The picture of a chair is certainly more restricted than the word 'chair', which, in its generic form, leaves almost everything open to the imagination.

Gutenberg's winepress

One has only to think of the paucity of words used in Japanese haiku in contrast to its depth of feeling and allusion, to see that a limited vocabulary can sometimes be the source of multiple streams. It was no mistake that Gutenberg's first printing press was adapted from a winepress. One must squeeze the words to their utmost in order to extract the poetry from them.

Dignity

Ultimately there is but one audience. The writer must write for himself. He must try to free himself from the winds of opinion that blow him this way one day and that way another. The writer must constantly return to the spontaneity of the act itself, the dignity and joy must be found there. To return to the creative impulse, to work without hope or fear of praise or calumny is indeed dignified. It is a life's work, a struggle more important than any particular book or essay, more important than any passing criticism or hyperbole.

Aphorisms 2

If a machine produces sounds, such as white noise, that are extraneous to its intended function, those sounds are a sign that the machine is wasting energy.

'The willing suspension of disbelief' has given way in our times to 'the willing suspension of privacy'.

A work of art should be resistant to analysis, for it is not a concoction of chemical elements whose nature can be deduced by tearing it apart.

Myth (1)

If 'homo ludens' is the being that plays, then it can be surmised that much of that play is taken up with the telling of tales, or the making of myths. As human beings, one of our major preoccupations is the invention of myths. It is perhaps our essential activity, that which defines us as human. When man first dipped his fingers in the mud and drew on the cave wall, that sign was meant to outlast the call of the voice, was meant to invent a myth that would continue beyond an echo.

Roland Barthes points out in *Myth Today*, "myth is a type of speech," which certainly echoes the etymological sources. The word 'myth' finds its root in the Greek '*muthos*', meaning speech or narrative. This can be traced back to the Indo-European root, '*mud–*', to think, to imagine. How strange that the word is 'mud', with its suggestion of our mythical beginnings in fecund clay.

No matter what our approach to reality, no matter what concepts and words we use to contain the chaos of our world, we invent myth. We might call it materialism, religion, science, love, God, power or the absurd. Nonetheless, it is myth. It might be the myth we have chosen to believe. It remains, nonetheless, myth. And not necessarily a lie or an illusion, but perhaps a workable approach to the world. Myth, at its best, is our way of functioning, our means of bringing order to chaos. It is also our way of describing to ourselves what it is we are doing.

Impossibility of the new

While reading a description of the countryside, it occurs to me that it is utterly impossible to picture a scene entirely new. I keep harking back to rural scenes from memory and putting them in place of the description. Perhaps this is true of everything we read – no characters but those who spark memories of real people (and parts of real people in new combinations) that we once knew or met, or glimpsed for a moment. No houses but those we have visited, remembered, disassembled, reconstructed with the structures of memory. No happy experience, or sad, that was but an echo.

The attraction, then, of reading and writing must be the infinite multiplicity of possibilities. The memories fragmented and rebuilt into meaningful narrative, the endless play of phenomena in all its guises, not unlike the twenty-six letters themselves (and a space), arranged and rearranged in patterns to replicate the song of the songbird, the shot of an arrow, the curve of the moon.

Map

I once knew a man, a writer, who hated books. He hated libraries too. I found this difficult to understand until I realized that he found books and libraries to be an affront – all those possible worlds had been removed from him, they were worlds he could no longer create himself, but could only take as pabulum from another's imagination. He was like an explorer who sets out to explore a new land and, the day he is to leave, discovers a map has already been made of the world he hoped to reveal.

The letter E

The precursor of the letter E is the image of a calling or praying figure. This image can be seen in the letter E turned on its flat edge, in which the middle line represents the figure's head while the two outer lines are the upraised arms.

This most common of vowels, when voiced in full, sounds like a cry to the heavens. Picture the Phoenician priest, intermediary between heaven and earth, as he sings praise to the gods, his mouth open, his droning cry echoing still in today's muezzin or cantor, echoing off the Wailing Wall in Jerusalem where the faithful write their requests to the Omnipotent on bits of paper they then stuff into cracks in the stones.

Myth (2)

When one envisions the self-reflective quality of myth, one can walk into it and disappear. One can look into the mirror and discover that the mirror and the agent create each other, even as the reflective mind and the phenomenal world create each other.

The result is an emptiness that throws the world into sharp relief. As light plays on the senses, it reveals a world that creates itself *as* we imagine it. Naming things is just one stage in this process. Naming things is both a control on the incipient chaos (always ready to reassert its hegemony) and a possible deadening factor.

By this I mean that names can place themselves between the imagination and the thing. The imagination can become dulled and start to believe that the things are their names. The senses atrophy. The names themselves atrophy because they are no longer connected to living presences.

When the thing (the object) is sensed thoroughly, utterly, then the name fits. The object comes alive in its name. The name is a perfect emanation of what the object embodies. This is why it was said of Merlin that when he spoke the word 'fish' or the word 'snow', fish and snow would appear in the air or water. This is the ultimate power and secret of language, its power over the mind. The mind is the sixth sense, what it senses is words.

Books and place (1)

I finished reading Samuel Beckett's trilogy of novels – *Molloy, Malone Dies, The Unnamable* – on the beach beside a small lake in rural Vermont. It had taken me the better part of two years to read the 414 pages of the Grove Edition, not because I wasn't taken with Beckett's obsessions but because I was forced to savour his intensity in small doses. The complexity of those internal worlds was not something I could appreciate in all moods. Beckett is, if nothing else, and here especially, unrelenting.

So it was I took the book on vacation. ("Keep going, going on, call that going, call that on.") I found myself in the most common of situations, with wife and son on a summer beach crowded with other vacationers and locals. I read the last thirty pages there, but the rest of the book was still with me, I had lived and breathed its tortured, honest passages, its profound meditations on death and existence. When I came to the last lines – "…it will be the silence, where I am, I don't know, I'll never know, in the silence you don't know, you must go on, I can't go on, I'll go on" – I was deeply touched by Beckett's complete openness and humanity, his willingness to express the truth and ambiguity of the human predicament. There among the bathers, the chaotic choir of summer voices, the kids splashing in and out of the water, in the middle of a fine sunny day, I wept, openly and without care, I wept for myself, for those around me, for Beckett himself who felt so deeply, for all humans. I thought about the silence and wept.

Light

What is this stuff we call light? We know at least something about the scientific explanations, the sparkle of photons, the play of particles. We all recognize the spill of sun, the cold white rain of stars, the cool fountain of the moon. But what is it really?

We use the term 'to enlighten'. To bring light upon a subject, to reveal it. Surprisingly, the traditional four elements – earth, air, fire, water – do not include light although light can appear in all of them. Light obviously is of the essence in air and fire. As for earth and water, light can appear not only as a reflection from a still lake or a slab of mica, but also as glowing phosphorescence.

I once awoke in my cabin in the Gatineau Hills of western Quebec in the middle of the night. Rather than light a lamp, I made my way downstairs in the familiar dark and headed for the front door, hoping to release my bladder outdoors under the frothy cascade of the Milky Way. As I passed the woodbin piled with logs, I noticed a glow and went to the window seeking the moon, which I figured must have been the source of the light. Much to my puzzlement, there was no moon. Returning to the woodbin, I stared at a log glowing with phosphorescence, a strange soft steady light. In ten years living in that cabin, in ten years of handling, literally, a mountainside of logs, I never before or again saw phosphorescence. By the next night, it was gone, burned out in its living impermanent way.

But what of light? From the calm grey sky, blowing through the trees in the morning, singing from the desktop lamp. I remember light glowing, lambent and rich, from the face of a friend on his wedding day. I recall the way the meditation hall turned brighter and brighter gold as the Tibetan teacher approached in slow procession.

Writing of light always sounds more prose-poem than essay. It is that diaphanous. Can't put your finger on it. Shining up from a lake at noon. Passing at odd angles through the windows of an Airbus.

I remember someone saying: "I love to meditate on sunny days." This seemed odd until I stopped thinking about it.

We value light. At my former office on the nineteenth floor, one's position in the corporation could be measured by one's closeness to the windows.

We hunger for light. Especially here in Ottawa, coldest capital city in the world, where the light disappears by 4:30 on a winter's afternoon.

Lucky the crazy light-drunk tern who migrates from Arctic to Antarctic, going back and forth with the midnight suns.

Light's eye draws the straight edges of the house, draws up the tree spiraling heavenward.

But what of the light within? The one that, no matter the depth of darkness surrounding it, can still be found. A steady, cool-burning phosphorescence without external source.

Books and place (2)

Sometimes a book is like a river – or a bus ride. I read *The Autumn of the Patriarch* by Garcia Marquez on the Ottawa city bus each day on my way to work as a consultant at the Bell Canada offices downtown. I would have approximately thirty minutes to read as the bus wound its way through rush-hour traffic. *The Autumn of the Patriarch*, a profile of a tyrant and his death in an unnamed South American country, is written using extremely long sentences (some go on for pages), no paragraph markings, and with an intensity and unity that can be compared to the flow of a great river that reflects the fetid jungles lining its shores.

Each day, when I took my seat on the bus, I would submerge myself again in that river of words, always the same river, but never quite the same river (like the fecund, complex repetition of the alphabet or, indeed, our daily lives). The river of words resembled the bus trip I took over and over again, every morning, in the flow of daily traffic. The river going on, always the same, always changing.

Myth (3)

Because life reveals itself to us as a tale unfolding, the arrangement of the words evolves into the arrangement of the narrative (or incidents). We imagine it, we 'signify' it, we decide what is 'significant'. Myth is not, as some claim, the mystery of the unknowable. Myth is the process of spontaneously deciding what is significant.

And yet, we are dissatisfied with this, for it implies a kind of closure, a narrowness to myth. We go back to the word: myth also finds its root in the Lithuanian 'maudzu' or 'mausti', to yearn for. There persists an element of longing in this way we imagine our world, a longing to reach beyond the limits of the self, to open to the world. The more one opens to the world, the more possibilities there are for finding significance.

For the narrow imagination, significance is found only in the churn of daily life. A kind of myth, nevertheless. The narrow imagination finds significance only in those events that affect itself – love, success, family, fear, money, fame, illness, death, and so on.

The imagination could open to the possibility of absolute significance. No decision need be made. The effort of deciding what is significant is dropped. All is significant. All remains, nevertheless, empty. Only against an absolute emptiness can an absolute significance be revealed. We are not necessarily talking about 'meaning' but 'connectedness'. All acts, all objects, are understood as expressions of coincidence. The world meshes. For the open imagination, the mirror and the agent are coincident, the mind and the phenomenal world are coincident. The names spontaneously arise as the coincident voice.

Alphabetization

During the Middle Ages, medieval intellectuals decided to construct library catalogues in a way that would make it easier for someone seeking a certain document or specific information. They abandoned the old order based on relative religious importance in which, in all catalogues and indices, the Bible came first, the writings of the Church Fathers second, other religious texts followed. The liberal arts came at the end.

To replace this system, they chose alphabetization based simply on the first letter of a word. In this library, as in a modern day index or dictionary, everything is of equal value – God and King appear as equals of apple, manna and yew tree. This is a major, if subtle, step in breaking down traditional ways of seeing the world. It speaks of the importance of order as an abstract concept. It rings of science and mathematics in which every number, every digit, is equal in importance for conveying information.

In another subtle way, it speaks too against poetry, and belies the view that all of reality is based on an overarching or root story, whatever that *ur* story might be. It also begins to break down the distinction between the secular and the sacred. It says, "Everything is equal here, nothing outweighs anything else."

The letter H

Befitting its heavily aspirated quality, the precursor of the letter H is a fence – not quite solid as a wall but not an open field either. In the beginning, H was depicted on its side with several more interstitial lines. Today, the fence has been turned on end, making it a ladder with a single rung. Is it mere coincidence that we have been moving steadily over the past several thousand years from a horizontal, rural perception to a more vertical, urban reality – from open field and one-storey house to skyscraper and office tower?

Myth (4)

For the open imagination, time holds no meaning. The narrative of the myth continually creates itself and continually dissolves. In a sense, there is no narrative. The voice dissipates in the air, the mud fades from the cave wall. In another sense, a narrative can be intuited – we can hear the echo of the rhyme in the rhythm of the voice, we can read the tale in our palms, on the cave wall, against the night sky, in books. The possibility of narrative and the possibility of no narrative are the two sides of the mirror. They constantly pass through each other. This is how we weave the two halves of our world together, on the loom of emptiness and fullness, on the loom of meaning and the meaningless.

Roland Barthes suggests that poetry is "the search for the inalienable meaning of things" and that one is left to "poetize" when reality is "ultimately impenetrable, irreducible." In other words, the poet is forever stuck mouthing the unspeakable, beating the dead horse of mystery. This perception helps explain the low standing of poetry in our world today. Technocracy has eroded the standing of mystery (or it believes it has). The particular myth of the rational technocratic mind has relegated poetry to the back burner. Of course, rationalism, the prevailing idiom (it *is* a way of language) refuses to see itself as myth. To myth it opposes truth or fact, seeing myth as the invented and itself as the real. There remains no room for mystery, no room for what is considered to be poetry.

I disagree thoroughly with this understanding of poetry as the opposite of non-mystery (or what Barthes terms 'ideology'). Mystery is *not* the realm of poetry. Nor is ideology. Neither superstition nor reason. The terms themselves must be denied. They are two possibilities, two forms, of myth. They create each other.

In a spontaneously arising invention of the world, poetry is the emanating voice, another expression of the form, as real as smell or taste. The name 'pear' means as much to mind as pear sweetness means to the tongue, as pear scent means to the nose. In this world, there is no conflict between reason and poetry, between ideology and mystery. Each has its use. In the pure coincident function of myth, there is no need to decide between them. Neither is more significant than the other. Both are empty and utterly rich and full. Both are forms of myth.

Wind

I sit on the backyard deck at home on a warm July evening and contemplate the invisible wind. The four houses whose backs I can see on the next street have high trees beyond them – maples, ash. The wind, gusting from the west, moves through the first tree, then the lower second, then the high full third. But, it's not that simple – because winds have multiple heads and long lingering tails. I discover by watching closely that they have width, length and height also.

There is nothing linear about them. They flow through the high trees, they stiffen the neighbour's flag – red maple leaf on a white ground. They swirl through the side neighbour's tall white pine, then trickle off, skirling backwards or circling, through the two little apple trees in my own yard, through the sumac behind the shed and beyond.

Meanwhile another wind comes through the venerable bittersweet vine shading the deck and tosses the green leaves of the not-yet-blooming morning glories.

The wind seems to have intelligence. It appears to be alive, an animal of air.

The winds are warm and delicious. We recognize them solely by their effect, by how they move the world. Another just now circled from sumac to apple tree to second apple to tall thin plum tree to morning glory vines to bittersweet, and disappeared or perhaps died.

Do winds die? Quickly and without complaint.

Myth (5)

In the myth that sees itself imagining itself, there is no mystery. There is a kind of magic nonetheless. Not the magic of gods, not the magic of demons, but a quite ordinary human magic. The ability to hear the names of things is a kind of magic, to know that the names are not tacked on afterwards but are the perfect expression of the things, coincident with them, arising as they arise. This magic aspect of language can only exist coincident with the realization of the emptiness of language, language being empty because it is pure construct; that is, sounds have been chosen to represent things. (The sound 'door' has nothing to do with the object 'door'.)

There appears to be a contradiction here: language as construct versus language as magical expression or incantation. But this contradiction is more apparent than real. In fact, language as perfect emanation depends on the knowledge of language as construct. This understanding of language is magic without mystery, a clear and apparent magic available when we see that we invent the world as we go.

This text, too, does not escape being a form of myth. To believe it is to believe in a myth. To deny it is to believe in another kind of myth. The mind creates the world as the world creates the mind. Which came first? Neither. Did emptiness come first then? No. In this particular invention, there is no 'coming first', for time too is a certain kind of myth.

The mind that reflects in these words was never born.

Vicarious living

A recent article in the *Globe and Mail* reported on a study that had been conducted on the willingness of people to come to another's aid. The study concluded that people who were less educated and those who were manual labourers were much more likely to come to the assistance of another human being in trouble than those who were highly educated or well-read.

Without any scientific proof, I believe this has something to do with the act of observation, of living vicariously. In some sense, vicarious living takes us out of life, turns us into spectators rather than participants. In another sense, this ability to be a spectator – to imagine life even as we live it, to reflect – is apparently one of the characteristics that makes us distinctively human.

At times it seems we live so much in the world of the mind and imagination that we can barely react when we see another's real suffering. We picture it happening outside us, as if we were watching a film or reading a story. I fervently hope that this theory is incorrect.

Possession and exorcism

We are "possessed" by our own minds; we are in need of exorcism. Although we believe we possess our minds it is the mind that thinks this. The mind appears to be a demon that through the power of habit and repetition "possesses" the totality of the human being. Language and thinking are its primary tools, its ultimate drugs. Religion may have been the opiate of the masses but it is language that is the opiate of Everyman.

We grow up being habituated to the language of our elders, formed to a certain inescapable shape in the image of our mothers, fathers, ancestors. Those who attempt to awaken from the demon of the mind are involved in a life of exorcism, an attempt to see through what has become the standard, the routine, the normal.

This is the role of the shaman in the modern world. To break free of possession, to exorcise oneself of the mind without losing the mind, to remain aware of the thin but real and definite line between the psychotic and the shamanic or sacred/ecstatic.

Taming language

We are possessed by our minds and crave exorcism. Language is the rope that binds us into place, the nail in the cross that fixes the transepts of duality.

With language and story, we project the world. We have imagined it, created it, defined it, limited it. It seems that we need to limit the world, our reality, in order to work with it. Language is an extremely useful tool, perhaps the most useful human tool ever invented, but in order to make it work for us we have first to tame it. And we *have* tamed it, brought it out of chaos, out of eternity into time, broken it into pieces that can be measured and used as building blocks to construct our world.

At the same time, we have gone too far in taming language, have taken away much of its energy out of fear that we would lose control over language and thus lose control of our minds and our world.

Thus when we use language, instead of employing it in ways that are fresh and open and creative, we instead "round up the usual suspects," grasp the words that most quickly and easily fit, rely on habitual tendencies to pattern our language in ways that are safe and non-threatening, harness or ignore our imaginations and make them walk in familiar ruts.

We need to tame language in order to use it, in order to communicate. But we must take care not to cage it, not to remove its life force, not to disengage its resplendent charge.

The letter K

Hold your left hand horizontally in front of you, palm facing in. Keeping all other fingers and thumb tight together, allow a space to open between the two middle fingers. There you have the letter K, originally a pictograph depicting the palm of the hand (the letter 'kaf' in Hebrew).

The sound of the letter K (like P) is quite distinct. It can be grasped, it must be grasped in order to be sounded. K, unlike P, is not projected, it is held in, it takes its place in the world, it stands its ground, it holds itself steady.

The palm of the hand swirls with deltas and rivers of time, one's life is written there in a language that some claim can be read. The same hand holds a pen, scribes lines on a sheet of standard 8 ½ x 11 paper whose size approximates the size of the human head.

Compressed creativity

A look at the timeline of Song Dynasty China (907-1279) reveals a stunning period of creativity, perhaps the most compressed instance of this in the history of mankind.

In a single twenty-one year stretch, from 1024 to 1045, four world-changing discoveries were revealed: paper money was invented, leading to the concept of credit; the compass was also invented, invaluable for travel and trade; moveable type was developed, leading to the easier dissemination of books and the knowledge and skills they contained. And finally, the formula for gunpowder was first published.

What made this explosion of creativity possible? It seems telling that the period in question was preceded by a significant increase in agricultural output, including new types of seed rice from Vietnam. This agricultural explosion was immediately followed by a significant population increase. By 1020, China's population surpassed one hundred million for the first time. The next twenty-five years would prove to be China's version of the Renaissance.

Aphorisms 3

When we meet the aliens, we will be meeting ourselves in another time.

To be at rest in the groundlessness of the great ambiguity is freedom.

The true radical never takes sides.

Gap

Horse moves, slightest of pauses, wagon moves. There is a gap between outbreath and inbreath, between the whippoorwill drawing in its breath and the start of the song; a gap when the pianist has already begun the concerto but no music has yet reached our ears; the gap between seeing lightning in the sky and the word 'lightning' appearing in the mind.

That moment of groundless indecision when you don't know if it's a star or a shooting star.

Writing systems

Jared Diamond writes in *Guns, Germs, and Steel*, "In the last centuries before 3000 B.C., developments in accounting technology, format, and signs rapidly led to the first system of writing." Diamond supports the commonly accepted view that the oldest writing systems were for the purpose of economics – to keep track of numbers of sheep and amounts of grain, to record trade and other transactions.

But what of the "writing" that appeared on Paleolithic cave walls twenty thousand years earlier? While we are familiar with the drawings of animals that decorate the caves at Lascaux, Altamira and dozens of other cave sites, Paleolithic caves also contain symbols and signs whose meaning we can only guess at but which can be considered a form of writing. These signs consist of + and X signs, and strokes and circles and so on. While many historians might think of these as meaningless cave graffiti, there is no valid reason to discount them as a form of written communication.

And perhaps even earlier, one can imagine the pre-agrarian hunter/gatherer making marks in the earth or on a stick to describe the number of wild animals and the directions in which they are located. The impermanence of these media (wooden sticks, the earth itself) means they have not survived in the same way as Sumerian cuneiform stamped in clay or Egyptian hieroglyphics cut in stone.

Perhaps it all grew out of storytelling. The need to share the story of how I wandered for two moons or seven suns in that direction (arrow drawn on the ground), and while I was there I saw three villages (circles drawn on the ground), and counted fourteen men, thirteen women and seventeen children (lines of various length) who live on a tuber we have never seen and who dance in strange ways.

Or perhaps it was an attempt by one of our earliest ancestors to account for what he or she saw during a vision quest or while walking alone across the empty savannah. Perhaps it was a story, a myth, about one of their gods.

The belief that the first writing was used for economics rather than some other purpose, such as magic, religion or storytelling, reveals a significant bias for economics in the view of historians.

Learned instinct

I'm not sure I can say this, not sure I can even think it, for it involves something I can see only, at times, out a corner of the eye, a thread of light so fine as to be easily lost in the sparking chaos, a mere scent come in a flash and just as quickly gone.

This moment of awareness is neither conscious nor unconscious, but at another level. You are not in control of it. It's in control but "it" isn't anything other than pure nameless awareness without anything to cling to, or to praise or to blame.

An example. While visiting a friend once, I began to roughhouse with his two rambunctious sons of eight and ten. I was paying attention to the eight-year-old when I turned to find the ten-year-old's fist heading for my sternum at a terrifying speed. My reaction was purely and deeply instinctual – no time to put my hands or arms up for protection, no time to duck, no time to move at all, no time even for fear. I think I simply watched, purely, without thinking. Without calling it up, in an instant, a kind of invisible power kicked in. When the boy's fist hit the center of my chest, I don't remember feeling anything but he was thrown backwards and knocked soundly to the floor. He looked up in amazement at me looking at him in amazement, neither of us knowing how this had happened.

Meditative practices are like that, I think. We can't *use* them, but they kick in – not when *we* think we need them, because that involves too much self-consciousness. But not at random either. They kick in at that moment when bone hits rock, like at the moment of death.

Writer as alchemist

The writer as alchemist must learn how to transcend hesitation and keep words on the bubble. He mixes elements in that inner room where the dreamer dreams alone. Imagination acts spontaneously, without scruples – until the alchemist intuits a thread, a direction that offers the possibility of open space, which is the locus of creation. He follows that line because he must. To refuse would be death. He goes there and dreams new beings.

Words of every description circle about his head: *clove, skin, anarchist, wellhead, flame, cascade, ardent*... Words bubble out of his imagination, wash up from the sea, are found echoing in ancient and as yet unwritten manuscripts, fall like rain, pass like gulls, gather like dust, words of the possible, already there in the empty wind.

With them, the alchemist constructs descriptions of the world, new realities, open visions. Out of the psychic chaos he forms new personalities and prepares them for birth. The writer engenders the marvelous, the strange, the star-crossed and profane. With the chiaroscuro of language, the writer as alchemist ruptures planes and slides through, drawing the reader after.

Another proof 1

It is precisely because He does *not* exist, that God could so utterly love the world. Absolute love demands the lover be completely empty of selfhood. Therefore God's love is entirely dependent on God's non-existence.

Amnesia

Amnesia is the consistent theme, our condition. We live in a state of semi-amnesia because we have forgotten far, far more than we remember. That's why we cling so desperately to our names, the names of things, afraid of forgetting, because we fear the emptiness, the silence, beyond names, beyond ourselves.

Mathematics and language

The essayist George Steiner has lamented the increasing importance and power of the language of mathematics in today's world, as well as the concomitant decline of the written word. The written word is considered vague by the modern technocrat, while mathematics and the vocabularies of science suggest a high degree of precision.

It is precisely due to its vagueness that the word is truer to life than the language of mathematics. Its chemical description is H_2O, but water is more than that. Water as an idea is endlessly rich in words and allusion – *wet, cold, black, silver, cascading, calm, reflective, deep, troubled*. Scientific language is narrow. Words are broad. Words include a kind of natural chaos and remind us of their own imprecision and the illusory nature of communication. Scientific language, that is to say, mathematics, pretends to be beyond illusion and yet is thoroughly enamored of the myth of reason. It believes its closed system is the world – a belief both highly deluded and effective.

This dream we dream

This dream we dream is a kind of language – not simply inexpressible but a language of inexpressibility.

Is this nothing more than a word-game? Yes, and to label it as a word-game is another kind of word-game, another kind of language.

The growing dawn

In a sense all literature is biography (or autobiography), speaking as it does of the lives of men and women, or of the life of the author. Even the most abstract treatise tells something of human relationships. In another sense, every biography is ultimately myth. The biographer draws lines between stars, constructs a figure, animates the silence.

The narrow line between two words splits the brain itself in half. What distinguishes myth from reality? What is fact and what is fiction? The world is as it is: beyond words, before words, after words. Yet, we choose not to live in silence.

The sciences, too, can begin to sound oddly like a new mythology. The lexicon of quantum mechanics includes terms such as quark, gluon, quink, beauty, bottom, charm, up, down and strange. The job of naming things has always been reserved for those who create, or discover, new worlds. What is fact and what is fiction or, for that matter, what is a fraction and what is friction?

Up down, all around, strange beauty.

The British physicist, Sir James Jeans, once said: "Today there is a wide measure of agreement, which on the physical side of science approaches almost to unanimity, that the stream of knowledge is heading towards a non-mechanical reality; the universe begins to look more like a great thought than like a great machine."

Words too have their lives, their histories, their biographers. Exposing the roots of words reveals a mythopoeic structure beneath language, a past that is not lost but is the actual hidden foundation of the present. In the mechanics of mind, the word plays the role of the atom: break the words open, release the light.

Choosing fate

Fate and free will are one and the same. Somehow, we choose our fate. The next moment is totally unpredictable, but when the bird calls, or the hammer cracks, or the plane passes overhead, it is as if that had been waiting to happen, as if the world had taken its proper place, as if these events fit perfectly into slots already awaiting them. And then it happens again, in the next moment – it has a continuity, entirely unpredictable but utterly correct. It doesn't 'mean' anything – it just is, without any suggestion of a divine plan. And it's not 'fixed'.

These words, this description, is likely an attempt to 'fix' it, to pin it down – but the world moves on to its next moment. Fate's wheel turns in whatever direction we choose. We just have to get out of the way.

A well-designed, beautiful theory

It is said among scientists that a well-designed, beautiful theory will be "simple, compact and spare; it will give a sense of completeness and often an eerie sense of symmetry" (Charles Seife, *Zero*). The same can be said of a well-designed, beautiful novel or a well-designed, beautiful poem.

A certain kind of truth

Newspapers and other mass media offer a certain kind of truth – one that is bound by convention and limited beliefs about reality.

Creativity, on the other hand, is about lying. The Creative knows and admits it is lying (fiction is lying even as it can be a version of the truth), whereas the media believe that their truth, their version, is 'the' truth, the only truth, the whole truth.

Humans are perhaps not capable of the whole truth. (This too is a version.)

The letter M

The original pictograph for the letter M was an image of water. The visual connection is obvious but the sound connection is also intriguing. M, the 13th and middle letter of the alphabet, is the deep "mmmm" my computer intones at this moment. M is the sound of machines; its consistent, steady aspect suggests the stream or river. I picture the current (liquid and/or electrical) flowing with the letter M in ripples and waves.

For the ancient Chinese, streams and rivers symbolized the mind, which never ceases flowing and is endlessly fertile. The mountain, in its vast stillness, stood as a symbol for the heart.

Social consensus

Given: Language is based on consensus, a mutual agreement that certain sounds have certain meanings. Our perception of reality, too, is based on mutual agreement, a deeply felt consensus of which we are barely conscious. This is an extremely limiting restriction on consciousness. When we unwittingly step outside this agreement and create another reality in which we believe, we could be considered insane. If we can *knowingly* step outside this consensus, and still function effectively within it, we can escape some of the power of this fundamental restriction. This locale is known as the playground of the creative.

Unavoidable

Beware when a great subject becomes a great project. Artists should not create 'art for art's sake', nor should they create solely for the sake of politics or religion. Creation should be for the sake of something broader, deeper and longer than politics, religion, or even art itself. The creative act should be undertaken because it is unavoidable, because something deep inside one 'insists'.

Duchamp 1

Duchamp used a piece of glass as a palette – red, blue, green, yellow – the same seen from either side.

The past and future look pretty much the same from here. We have a saying: *What goes around comes around.* Any way you hold the palette of time, you can look clear through it and see what's in your hand.

Duchamp also had this thing about 'breaking even'. He applied it, first and foremost, to economics, believing that one should earn about as much money as one needs to live.

Breaking even is more than just a Duchampian approach to economics. It reflects life itself: You're born, you die. Even Steven. No getting around it. The accumulation of capital cannot help you avoid eventual bankruptcy. Even the sun will burn out someday. Maybe the universe is half light and half dark, although the astronomers will tell you it's a lot darker than that. But they haven't been everywhere, like inside Duchamp's head, where a palette of glass shimmers, floating in the air, its yellow green blue red visible both ways.

Music and language

The idea that music is an art form superior to language is an insupportable cliché. It is a belief held by many writers and critics (not Joyce) and most musicians, of course.

Language at its height is a pre-mathematical music, a pre-notational music, a system that contains its own structures and rules within each line, paragraph, stanza, story.

One could say, music is easy, language difficult, and vice-versa. To find the meaning in music can be difficult, while the meaning in language is usually apparent (but not always). To find the music in language can be difficult, while the music of music is obvious.

Duchamp 2

In late 1911 or early 1912 Marcel Duchamp made a sketch of a nude *ascending* a staircase. Later, when he began work on the painting for which the sketch was intended, he decided to depict the nude *descending* the staircase. In that moment the theme of the modern age changed, the myth of progress was exposed and modernism began its long descent into doubt.

In Duchamp's mind, the nude turned and came down, which normally would suggest a dynamic moment, a moment of entry, the nude muse offering herself to the artist, to the world. But there persists a sense that the height had been attained and everything was downhill from there. The descent had begun.

The letter N

A serpent or snake was the original pictogram of the letter N. Once again the visual connection is apparent although most people tend to find the serpent in the letter S. (Snake-like demons in Tibet are called nagas.)

Many of the uppercase letters have been "squared" over the past several thousand years. It is certainly easier to chisel square capitals in stone than a line of cursive. Uppercase N has lost its sinuous quality, as have uppercase A, M and numerous others.

The ecstatics of language

The art is not ours – we are possessed by it, and like the shaman we are a conduit for the greater, wider life (not some god or demon we are channeling). It, meaning the art and the life, is neither cruelty nor pleasure (see Artaud); it neither exists nor does it not exist. It is eternal flux and does not admit of the logic of language. It does admit, however, of the ecstatics of language.

Aphorisms 4

History is nothing but stories.

In the history of the New World, the Spanish got all the gold and the English got beaver hats.

Nothing to be done as you turn to stone dust air light.

All-ee-all-ee-in-free

All the words ever uttered have collected in a band high in the atmosphere. Trapped, copious as hydrogen. Once in a while a word, a phrase, may be drawn out along some elemental line of force into space, to begin its wandering voyage to other realms, to become an enigma, a mystery in some other order of language. What could possibly be meant, the aliens will ask themselves, by *curling iron*? Or *wild pitch*? Or *all-ee-all-ee-in-free*?

Time unhinged

Nothing can be retrieved from the past, no matter how recent or distant. The actions, the people, the sounds of three minutes ago are as irretrievable as those of a hundred, a thousand, thirty-thousand years ago.

The future presents a similar problem. It is as difficult to see five minutes ahead as it is to see five thousand years ahead.

And where is the present? A shooting star zipping from one void to another. Impossible to catch.

Alternative versions

A quote from *Midnight's Children* by Salman Rushdie: "1001, the number of night, of magic, of alternative realities – a number beloved of poets and detested by politicians, for whom all alternative versions of the world are threats."

There is nothing but alternative versions of the world. (This too is an alternative version.)

The letter R

With a bit of imagination, somewhere in the letter R can be seen the human head (its pictographic source), perhaps in profile. R is the letter of radiance, while the head is the seat of power and the source of light. When we say someone is aglow, we mean they glow from the face. Perhaps there is some connection to Ra, the Egyptian sun-god.

Molly Bloom

We just might know the characters in novels more intimately than our family, acquaintances and friends because we know what they are thinking. Through the medium of the author (a 'medium' makes contact with the dead), we are privy to the internal dialogue of a character, the most private thoughts that they would never express to anyone in the outside world.

In some ways, I might know Molly Bloom better, more intimately, than my own mother.

Martin Guerre reconsidered

The Wife of Martin Guerre, published by Janet Lewis in 1941, is based on a real-life account from the annals of 16th century French law. The story was later resurrected as a film titled *The Return of Martin Guerre* starring Gerard Depardieu.

On one level, the story is a simple tale, a tragedy, of deceit and loss among the Languedoc peasantry. On another level, one could read the tale as a symbol of time's deception.

Martin Guerre has left his wife, Bertrande, for the ever-present wars down in the valleys. Eight years later another man, his double, returns to the village and claims to be Bertrande's husband.

At first Bertrande believes him but her doubts grow over the years until finally the deception is revealed.

This is what happens as we journey through time. The one you married changes, grows old, literally turns into a different person. Bertrande clings to an illusion and refuses to recognize the truth of time, the truth of change.

On this symbolic level, Martin Guerre never really left. The years simply went by, the seasons unfolded one into the next and the young husband she knew was gone forever. Another man, an imposter, moved into his body. This was a change Bertrande could not accept. Even hanging the imposter could not bring back her Martin as she knew him. He was gone forever.

The English Patient reconsidered

The story of Michael Ondaatje's *The English Patient* is the story of culture's catastrophe at the end of World War II. The ruins of the villa where the English patient has been brought to die are the ruins of our civilization.

In the novel, Ondaatje describes at length the half-collapsed structure, how it was exposed to the weather, how it was both inside and outside at once. Elemental nature was reasserting its hegemony over civilization, invading the decaying rooms of the world, even as nature, in the guise of death, was invading the English patient himself.

In the film, the ruinous aspect of the villa appeared to be significantly downplayed. Also downplayed was the crumbling personality of Hana, the nurse. In the film, Hana is little more than a sympathetic ear for the patient's tale. In the book she is half-mad, crazed with shellshock as well as the images and memories of the death and destruction around her. The character of Hana adds to the theme that the world as we know it is fracturing and falling apart. And I believe Ondaatje is referring not just to the war and the postwar period but to our own times as well.

A significant scene in the novel that perhaps is the most germane to the theme of civilization's collapse never appears in the film. When Kip, the Sikh sapper, hears on his crystal headset of the bombing of Hiroshima, Ondaatje's theme finds its most salient point. The end of the world through man's own madness is possible for the first time. And how pertinent that this news comes to the character of Kip first – a man who defuses bombs but who never had the opportunity to defuse this one.

We are still attempting to come to some understanding of the twenthieth century and its ultimate horrors – the holocaust, seventy million dead in the core of Europe, Hiroshima. In the words of essayist George Steiner, that period 'presses on the brain with a new darkness'.

Civilization, our world, had become that slab of roasted flesh on its bed. We are, have been ever since, ourselves, the English patient.

The letter S

The original pictogram that evolved into the letter S was the image of a bow. Notions and suggestions of fertility surround the letter. S is the letter that makes words plural. In English, more words begin with S than with any other letter. On my computer keyboard, I notice that the most-worn letter is S and this makes me wonder if, on old typewriters, the steel character S at the end of its typebar would wear out before others.

A bow too has ancient connections to fertility. An old term for 'fertile' is to have 'two strings to one's bow'.

Story as ritual

There is no narrator, no narrator at all. Although he may from time to time think he exists, he will be mistaken. Every story arises from fertile emptiness, dwells for a moment or two, and disappears into thin air. A breath.

It is patently ridiculous for me, the writer, to try to convince you, the reader, to pretend the story is actually happening, now, in some world concocted of a "willing suspension of disbelief." This is fine for children, but are you so easily tricked, so willingly made a fool? What then of 'story'? you may ask. What, precisely, is the point? *Not escape*, I would answer, *not fantasy*. How could I pretend that you don't have Hiroshima, Bergen-Belsen and other codes of our time permanently fixed at the back of your mind, how pretend that you are not, this moment, hearing the throb of traffic, the seductive whisper of the television commercial from the other room. I'm surprised you have space in your mind for these words at all. No, 'story' has nothing to do with a "willing suspension of disbelief."

Stories that counted, from the very beginning, were always about ritual. In escape or fantasy, repetition of the same story is ruinous, deadening. In ritual, repetition is the point, the words welling up as a form of magical incantation, gaining depth with each reading. The importance of ritual and repetition is found in the fact that it is the reader who changes, not the story, the reader who, like the narrator, does not exist at all.

Hallucination

In North America, it appears we live in a desert while hallucinating that we inhabit a world of plenty. Our groceries may be well stocked with meat, fish, fruit and vegetables but these comestibles are often laden with chemicals, brightly coloured as plastic, suspiciously bloated and tasteless. Several years ago, when Italian plum tomatoes first became available at my local grocery chain, they were fairly small and actually tasted like tomatoes. Now, they are twice the size they used to be and have lost a good deal of their taste. Commercially available spinach today apparently contains approximately twenty percent of the nutrients it did fifty years ago.

In many agricultural regions, the soil is dead and will only produce with the help of commercial fertilizers, and seeds are no longer the carriers of life but a product to be altered for the maximizing of profit.

A few years ago, a Canadian travel writer visited a market in Tashkent, the capital of Uzbekistan, and reported finding an astounding variety of fruits and vegetables in this poor region of the world. The market offered a hundred varieties of cherries, ten kinds of peaches, seven or eight types of watermelon, a dozen kinds of berries he had never before seen, and an astounding two hundred varieties of grapes. In North America, we are lucky if we can find four different kinds of grapes on grocery shelves and often we find only two, green and red. Even in a place like Italy, the grapes and other fruits have far more taste than in North America and the food in general tastes fresher and less bloated with chemicals and water.

I would not for a moment romanticize the hard lives of farmers in Uzbekistan or other rural localities around the world, but, in many ways, it is we who live in a shiny desert and hallucinate a world of richness.

The new

In his critique of Baudelaire in the *Arcades Project*, Walter Benjamin refers to the French poet's belief in "the inestimable value of novelty. *La nouveauté* represents that absolute which is no longer accessible to any interpretation or comparison."

Benjamin goes on to explain that this very 'newness' was "the ultimate entrenchment of art" and "commodity's most advanced line of attack." In other words, newness (we can say it applies to anything that is 'in fashion') was where art met the market and was instantly seduced and co-opted by it.

He adds that death, "the final voyage of the flaneur (the wanderer)," has the new as its destination.

The problem here is that as soon as the new is expressed or exposed, it is interpreted, it is no longer beyond interpretation. The new quickly gives birth to the old, the new becomes the habitual. But the absolute new that is truly beyond interpretation, that is beyond habit, gives birth to the new over and over. Actually, it doesn't give birth to any thing at all but is, in fact, the act of giving birth, of creating. The new (like any subatomic particle) is a verb, not a noun. There is nothing to interpret because nothing truly happens – concept has nothing to hold to, define or interpret because the new has already moved on – to the next new, and the next, and the next.

Stations of the Cross

Contrary to popular opinion, the first 'moving' picture was not an early stuttering black and white film but The Stations of the Cross. This is true because the worshipper/viewer is not separate from the object viewed – just as a scientist cannot truly be separate from his experiment and no viewer of art can be entirely separate from a work of art. With the Stations, the viewer is expected to move about the church from image to image. Furthermore, the Stations are filled with suggestions of movement and motion: walking, falling, climbing, hammering and so on. (Even the term 'stations' is intriguing.)

With the advent of film and television, the viewer is not expected to move but to be still and simply watch and observe. One walks about an art gallery or museum, but one sits down in a cinema. If viewer and object viewed are taken as a unified totality, then nothing has changed with technology except the object in motion.

Wonder

Polish poet Adam Zagajewski writes in *Another Beauty*: "The greatest artists of our age…acted as if they wanted to annihilate the forms of art they practiced. Picasso worked to destroy art, Stravinsky went after music, while Joyce's target was the novel." Perhaps this sense of annihilation of a form was necessary to create something original in that form. They felt they must destroy the stale approaches that preceded them before they could begin anew.

Zagajewski also writes, in the same volume: "Art springs from the most profound admiration for the world." The word 'admiration' has a fascinating etymology. Its family of words includes miracle, mirage, mirror, marvelous and smile. The Indo-European root for all these words is *mei*, 'I smile', and they also find their root in the Latin *mirus*, 'astonishing, strange, wonderful'. 'Admiration' comes, more specifically, from the Latin *admirari*, 'to wonder at'. Art, of course, is grounded in and springs from this sense of wonder. A sense of wonder does not necessarily suggest the 'extraordinary'; one can have a sense of wonder about the most 'ordinary' things: the waxy light reflected from a green pepper, the way the fellow at the corner gas station is always smiling and calls me 'boss', the pale blue winter sky between the clouds.

Evanescence

It's intriguing that poetry, that most evanescent of arts, lasts the longest of all cultural artifacts, while architecture, which one would expect to persist as long as the stones of the hills, tends to disappear relatively quickly from the face of the earth.

Thousands of poems of ancient China still exist, can be read today and, what is more astonishing, they can be understood. The poems that deal with the unchanging yet constantly changing world of nature are still extremely accessible, as opposed to those that reference the political world of their time. The four seasons still cycle around today as they did then, maples sprout leaves in the spring, the snow continues to fall each winter and catch in the boughs of the pines, and the mountains mentioned in ancient Chinese poems, while slightly more worn, are still recognizable.

Little remains today, however, of the architecture of ancient China (or any other ancient culture, for that matter, with the exception of enigmatic Egypt). What does remain are those edifices that have been brought low, literally: burial mounds and underground chambers.

Entire cities with their impregnable palaces have disappeared into dust and mist while a simple poem about the moon continues to shine.

Who do you think you are?

In *An Anthropologist On Mars*, Oliver Sacks discusses the nature of colour in his first chapter. He posits that colour is not out there, in the so-called real world, not a question of light's wave-length, but that colour is "constructed by the brain." By exploring the various ways in which radically injured brains adapt to circumstances, he discovers that it is the brain's role to create or construct "a coherent self and world."

Later, in a discussion of memory, Sacks references Gerald Edelman's view that "every perception is a creation, every memory is a re-creation."

Both these examples suggest that the nature of the self is far more malleable and 'constructed' than we normally believe. Like language, the self we have constructed, in any particular context, is based on an attempt to adapt to social consensus. We are driven by family, society and environment to be who we think we are. While this view is critical to survival, recognizing it as a survival instinct is a first step in realizing its limitations.

Wilderness

Is 'home' the opposite of 'wilderness'? No, for wilderness includes home. You could say wilderness transcends home, for wilderness suggests the eternal while home is temporary, this season's nest of twigs in an ancient tree.

We come from wilderness and we go back to it. Call it Big Home. It includes heaven and earth.

If you embrace wilderness, you can never be lost. If you can't see the forest for the trees, you will never find yourself. If you can learn to embrace wilderness, you will joyfully disappear into the double negative where home is wilderness and wilderness home and both form a nest made out of blue space.

Another proof 2

If there is a Creator, then he would most certainly 'create' like any other artist – that is, becoming entirely lost in the play of his creativity, to the extent that he forgets about his own existence. If God doesn't know that He exists, does He?

June evening under the bittersweet

On a June evening I'm sitting on the back deck after dinner underneath the bittersweet arbor. I feel as if I'm peering out from a green tent.

First I see a crow that lands on the telephone pole. Each time it caws, it puffs out its wings, a proud dramaturge dressed in a tuxedo on opening night.

I look at the little apple tree in the back yard. About fifteen feet high, it already has cherry-sized green apples on it, like Christmas decorations.

The tree offers what is revealed: its trunk, branches, leaves and fruit; and what is hidden: its root system – a world whose image only exists (for me, at this moment) in the imagination.

I stare at the little tree full of spring-green leaves, and I see its beauty, its glow. The way the apple branches twist and spiral out from the trunk, its fullness, its wholeness, its completeness. The way it reaches.

This contemplation fills me with a bittersweet feeling, for I can never quite fully describe how its branches and leaves move somehow together at the slightest breeze.

Aphorisms 5

Life has no punchline.

Reality consists entirely of footnotes for which we have no original text.

Nature has no opinion.

Opinions and celebration

What accounts for my low opinion of…opinions?

(I am well aware, of course, that this is another opinion, but life is rife with contradiction. We don't know where we come from, don't know where we are going, death follows life as surely as swallowing follows chewing, 'this' ends, ambiguity rules, and so on. This book too cannot avoid being a collection of opinions. Have I failed then? Yes, quite happily.)

Opinions are anti-celebratory. Celebration is inclusive, while opinions are always saying 'this is good, that is bad', 'I like pickles, I don't like fish'. Opinion is always weighing things, whereas celebration merely delights in them, even if it can also recognize them as failures. Opinion is so much 'what I think is…', 'what I believe is…', 'what I want is…'. Celebration looks out while opinion looks in, which means celebration sees more and further. Celebration doesn't always have to check back to head office to see if it's all right to enjoy life.

Writing should be a celebration: of stories, of life, of language. That is why most people today have forgotten how to enjoy poetry – they don't know how to enjoy language. They have too many opinions. They are so busy passing judgment, making their opinions known, that they can hardly breathe, breathing being essential to enjoyment, appreciation and celebration.

Godhead ad infinitum

If God created everything, then He must have created Himself, which makes for two Godheads. And the second, being God, must have created everything including Himself, which makes three Godheads. As you can see, this must go on and on with the result that there are infinite Godheads.

Chess backwards

Walter Benjamin writes (in the *Arcades Project*) of skilled chess enthusiasts in Paris who played with their backs to the chessboard. They were able to determine an opponent's move by the click of the piece on the board.

Consider the skilled poet. He knows the words of a poem about to be spoken by a fellow poet from the intake of her breath.

Consider the skilled shoemaker. He knows how to construct the required shoes by the sound of feet approaching his booth.

Consider the skilled confessor. He knows the sin by the ragged breath of the sinner.

Consider the confident king. He knows the requests of his charges by the depth and gracelessness of their bows.

Consider the open-hearted woman. She senses the needs of a man by the shine in his eyes.

And finally, consider the astute astronomer. He is drawn to discover a new star by the quality of blackness in a certain quarter of the sky.

Blank page

Ryszard Kapuscinski, in *The Soccer War*, writes of the way a desk can destroy the equality of human relationships. At a desk, one is higher, the other, lower; one is boss, the other, not. Only the Germans and Eastern Europeans can write so eloquently of office furniture. Heinrich Böll writes of a character in an office who is a slave to his telephones – he can speak into two at the same time, one in each hand.

The sheet of paper, too, like a desk, pronounces the limits of its rectangle. One is squeezed by its straight borders in four directions, like the borders of those flat Plains states, Iowa and Kansas. Kerouac tried to escape this restriction by feeding one long sheet through his typewriter, but there is still a limit – the long sheet remains one long rectangle.

Only the blank page offers the possibility of the infinite, the blank page with its pure emptiness announces endless depth, infinite possibility.

Organic

We have heard computer scientists speak of the possibility of organic computers, machines constructed of living material, able to grow.

We suggest the possibility of the organic novel, the organic poem or the organic myth, in which the chemical/molecular structure of the letters and words echo precisely their content (in terms of meaning), but with the further possibility that the tale those words tell can grow, evolve and change, thus taking the story into unforeseen realms.

Perhaps that is already happening. Perhaps that is what we are.

Acknowledgments

Selections from this collection first appeared, often in somewhat different form, in a variety of publications. They were published with the following titles:

Arc Magazine: "Pictographic Sources of the Alphabet as a Medium for Poetry;" "Myth and the Open Imagination"
Descant: "Copious as Hydrogen;" "Colourless green etc...;" "Organic Stories"
Numero Cinq: "Fragments of a story;" "Letters ubiquitous;" "Questions and answers;" "Language as social consensus;" "Sacred and profane;" "Troy imagined"

Several of the essays here were included in a lecture titled *Sacred & Profane* delivered at the Maritime Writers' Workshop at the University of New Brunswick.

"The growing dawn" first appeared as the Introduction to the novel, *The Growing Dawn*, published in 1983 by Quadrant Editions.

Many thanks for editorial suggestions to Nicola Vulpe, Chris Scott, and Allan Briesmaster. Any errors in fact (or fiction!) are mine alone.

Also by Mark Frutkin

FICTION
The Growing Dawn (1983)
Atmospheres Apollinaire (1988)
Invading Tibet (1991)
In the Time of the Angry Queen (1993)
The Lion of Venice (1997)
Slow Lightning (2001)
Fabrizio's Return (2006)

POETRY
The Alchemy of Clouds (1985)
Acts of Light (1992)
Iron Mountain (2001)

NONFICTION
Erratic North: A Vietnam Draft Resister's Life in the
Canadian Bush (2008)
Walking Backwards: Grand Tours, Minor Visitations,
Miraculous Journeys and a Few Good Meals (2011)

QUATTRO NOVELLAS